Using Science

by Jessica Quilty

Glenview, Illinois
Boston, Massachusetts
Chandler, Arizona
Upper Saddle River, New Jersey

Photographs
Every effort has been made to secure permission and provide appropriate credit for photographic material.
The publisher deeply regrets any omission and pledges to correct errors called to its attention in subsequent editions.

Unless otherwise acknowledged, all photographs are the copyright © of Dorling Kindersley, a division of Pearson.

Photo locators denoted as follows: Top (T), Center (C), Bottom (B), Left (L), Right (R), Background (Bkgd)

FP2 (TL) ©Bob Daemmrich/PhotoEdit, Inc., (BR) Getty Images.

Scott Foresman/Dorling Kindersley would also like to thank: 2 Natural History Museum/DK Images; 8 NASA/DK Images.

3 Corbis; 4 Franco Vogt/Corbis; 6 Hulton-Deutsch Collection/Corbis; 7 Getty Images; 10 Getty Images; 12 Getty Images; 14 Kevin Schafer/Corbis; 15 Roy Morsch/Corbis; 16 Getty Images; 18 Ariel Skelley/Corbis; 19 Getty Images; 20 (CR) Getty Images; 21 (TL) Honda; 22 Getty Images; 23 Getty Images, (BL) Michael A. Keller/Corbis.

ISBN-13: 978-0-328-61794-4
ISBN-10: 0-328-61794-6

5 6 7 8 9 10 V0FL 16 15 14 13

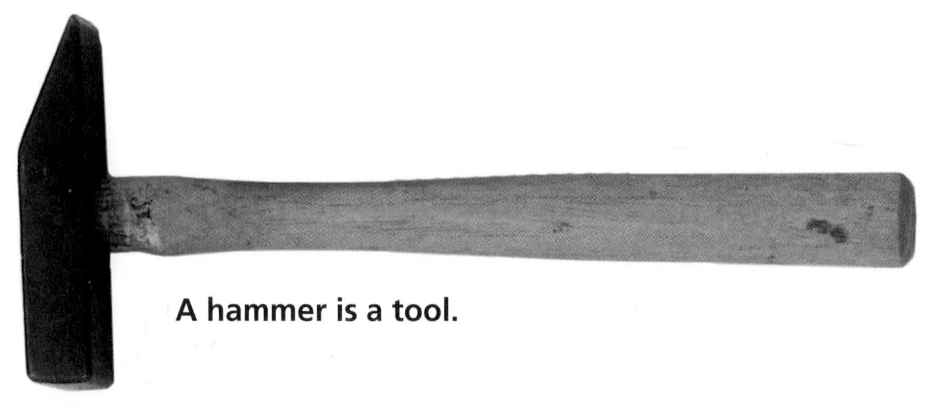

A hammer is a tool.

Technology In Our Lives

Ways to Improve

The United States was less than one hundred years old in the 1860s. Parts of the country still needed to be explored. Many people moved westward to do this.

But they still needed to communicate with people living in the East. People started thinking about how to do this. How could they communicate? Would a tool help? Was an invention needed?

Tools help people do jobs more easily. A tool can also help people think of new ways of doing things. **Technology** is the use of knowledge to create tools and ways of doing things.

People decided that an invention was needed to communicate. An **invention** is something created for the first time. The Pony Express was invented in the 1860s.

The Pony Express used horses and riders to carry mail across the country. This way, mail could be delivered between Missouri and California. Many riders and horses followed a schedule to move mail across the country. The invention of the Pony Express made communication between people living in the West and people living in the East faster.

New tools and technology are used to communicate today. Airplanes and other machines move mail around the whole world.

The Pony Express

Technology at Home

Many systems work together in your home. Just think about all the technology at work in your home every day. Your home is made up of walls and a roof. The walls are part of the framing system. The framing system works with the roofing system to protect your home from the weather. When you watch TV or play a video game, the electrical system is at work. When you wash your hands, the electrical system works with the plumbing system. These systems work together to bring you hot, running water.

A TV uses electricity.

The electrical system also helps you communicate. This technology makes it possible for you to use the telephone and the Internet.

How many telephones do you have in your house? Are the telephones the same or different? Some telephones have cords. Others are cordless. A cordless telephone can be taken all over your house.

Technology helps people keep in touch with each other.

Past, Present, And Future Technologies

Technology has affected many parts of modern life. Just think about transportation. Today people use cars. What types of transportation did people use before there were cars? A long time ago, people used horses and buggies to travel. But these types of transportation were slow. Many people also used trains. Trains and cars are very fast today. Sometimes you see superfast trains and cars in movies.

In the 1800s people traveled using horses and buggies.

Camera technology helps produce today's movies.

People have been enjoying movies for a long time. Many technologies are used in movies. Movies today are loud, exciting, and colorful. But the first moving pictures were silent. They were also black and white.

Soon, technology made color movies possible. This was very expensive at first. As technology improved, more movies were made in color. Before sound was added, people listened to live organ music during movies.

New Technologies

Extending Our Senses

Many people use technology in their jobs. Meteorologists are scientists who study the weather. One tool that helps them do their job is a weather satellite. Weather satellites orbit Earth. They have solar panels on them. The panels make power, so the satellites can take pictures or video. Then the satellites send the pictures or video of clouds, storms, and other weather back to Earth. There, meteorologists study the pictures. Then they can tell people what weather is coming. It's helpful to know if it's going to snow or rain so you can stay warm and dry.

Weather satellite

It is very difficult to see in the dark. But special technology makes this possible. People can use night vision goggles to see in the dark. These goggles use two different technologies. One technology uses heat. Objects, such as people, give off heat. The goggles sense the heat and create a picture from it. The other technology uses tiny amounts of light. People cannot see this light, but the goggles can detect it. Then they make an image from the light large enough for people to see.

Night vision goggles help people to see in the dark.

Sorting Information

You have probably noticed that computers are everywhere! A **computer** stores, processes, and sends electronic information really quickly. Computers make many parts of daily life easier. People use computers to sort and organize all kinds of information. You may use a computer to do your homework. Your school may use a computer to keep track of your grades. Your doctor may use a computer to record any sicknesses you have had.

Many people use computers at work.

MP3 players use computer chips. They allow people to download music from a computer.

Computer chips are used in many objects too. These tiny chips are found in MP3 players. People must use a computer to put music onto an MP3 player. Then they can take music with them wherever they go. The small player can hold hours of music. The computer chip inside makes it possible to organize the music. People can sort the music by their favorite songs, their favorite musician, or their favorite type of music.

Technologies for Moving Goods

Roads and highways are used every day. Our highway system makes it possible for people to travel. How do you get to school each day? You may ride a school bus. Or your parents may drive you. The bus and the car both travel on roads to reach your school.

People and goods travel on highways and on water.

Groceries can come from far away.

Millions of products travel on our roads and highways too. Some of the food found in grocery stores comes from far away. Sometimes people load food onto trucks at a farm. Other times people load it onto ships in other countries first. Then the food is loaded onto trucks. The trucks travel on highways to the grocery stores. Then people unload it. Finally, the food is put out in the store for people to buy.

Surprise Discoveries

Sometimes scientists and inventors are surprised by their results. Once in a while the results led to an unexpected discovery or new technology. Did you know bubblegum was a surprise discovery?

In 1869, Thomas Adams invented chewing gum. He made it out of a substance called chicle. Adams tried to use chicle to make many different things. He even tried to make bicycle tires out of it. Chewing gum became very popular. Many companies started making it. You could not blow bubbles with it though.

Chicle is sap from the sapodilla tree.

Walter E. Diemer worked for a chewing gum company called Fleer. Diemer was a businessman. But he liked experimenting with chewing gum recipes at home. In 1928, while working on a new recipe for chewing gum, he accidentally created a gum that stretched. Diemer realized he could even blow bubbles with it! This discovery became known as bubblegum. The first batch was pink because that was the only food coloring Diemer had. Most bubblegum today is still pink! For anyone who loves to chew gum and blow bubbles, this was a great surprise discovery.

Bubblegum

Technology And Energy

Using Energy

Think about how easy it is to use electricity today. If you need to use an electrical appliance, all you have to do is plug it into an electrical outlet. Then the energy is supplied. If you need to do some homework on a computer, all you need to do is turn the computer on. But it has not always been that easy.

For centuries people have burned wood to create heat for cooking and warmth. Although most people today use gas, oil, or electricity for these things, many still burn wood when camping.

Today coal, oil, and natural gas are burned to make heat and electricity. Dead trees, sawdust, and even paper products that cannot be recycled again can also be burned. This creates heat that can be used to make electricity.

Families cook on open fires when camping.

Producing Electricity

The resources of wind and water were used in the past to create energy. These resources are still used today, but in much different ways. In the past, a farmer often had one windmill on a farm. It used wind energy to do simple things, such as pump water. Today there are giant wind farms with lots of windmills. These new windmills use wind energy to create electricity.

Wind farms produce energy.

Waterpower is used to make energy.

People have been using the power of rushing water for a very long time. In the past, rushing water turned waterwheels. The waterwheels could power things, such as saws in lumber mills. Today, giant hydroelectric power dams are built to block river water. This water can be released. The rushing water turns modern waterwheels that make energy. Then this energy can be turned into electricity.

Technology and Energy Production

New technologies such as wind farms and hydroelectric power dams are very exciting. But they are also very expensive. Often, they do not create enough power and electricity for everyone to use. This means we still need to burn fossil fuels, such as coal or oil, at power plants. Burning these resources is less expensive and creates lots of power and electricity. However, burning fossil fuels also creates more pollution than many of the newer technologies.

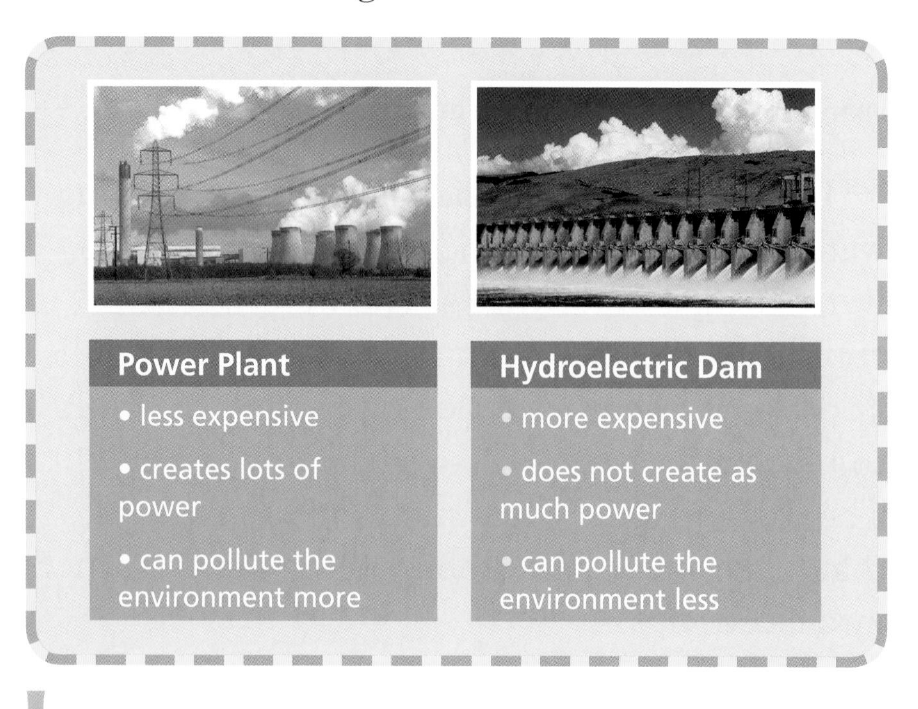

This hybrid car uses less gas and creates less pollution.

Scientists and inventors are working hard to find ways of creating power and electricity that are inexpensive, make enough electricity for everyone, and pollute the environment less. A car is a good example.

For a long time, most cars only used gasoline. But burning gasoline pollutes the environment. Today there are cars that use both gasoline and electricity. These cars are called hybrids. Some of the time they use gasoline, but other times they use electricity and create less pollution.

Why is technology important?

The role technology plays in changing our world is very important. Technology can be as simple as a hammer, or as complicated as a weather satellite.

The Pony Express made communication faster over long distances in the 1860s. Today technology in our home keeps us safe from weather, provides hot, running water, and helps us communicate. Technology has changed transportation in many ways. We have gone from horses and buggies to hybrid cars.

Technology has even improved entertainment. Movies today are amazing to watch because of sound, color, and special effects. Computers and computer chips have made MP3 players possible. All kinds of technologies are important!

MP3 players use computer chips to store information.

Glossary

computer	an electronic machine that can store, recall, or process information
invention	something made for the first time
technology	the use of knowledge to design tools and ways of doing things
tool	something used to do work